HISTORICAL ARCHAEOLOGY
AND THE LATTER-DAY SAINT PAST

HISTORICAL ARCHAEOLOGY AND THE LATTER-DAY SAINT PAST

Benjamin C. Pykles

LEONARD J. ARRINGTON
MORMON HISTORY LECTURE SERIES
NO. 27

Sponsored by
Special Collections & Archives
Merrill-Cazier Library
Utah State University
LOGAN

Copyright 2025

All rights reserved.

ISBN 978-1-64642-732-1 (paperback)

https://doi.org/10.5876/9781646427321

Published by Merrill-Cazier Library

Distributed by Utah State University Press

Logan, UT 84322

CONTENTS

ABSTRACT

At its core, archaeology is an effort to understand the human past through the study of the material remnants of that past. Although archaeology is often associated with the ancient world, the material remains that archaeologists study don't have to be thousands of years old. The branch of archaeology known as historical archaeology focuses on the more recent past, the last six hundred years of human history. This lecture reviews the history of archaeological investigations at sites connected to the Latter-day Saint past and examines the ways historical archaeology has contributed to our understanding of that past. Examples from various sites, where historical archaeologists have utilized a wide range of methods, illustrate the potential of historical archaeology to confirm, complete, correct, and sometimes confuse our understanding of the Latter-day Saint past.

HISTORICAL ARCHAEOLOGY
AND THE LATTER-DAY SAINT PAST

FIGURE 1. Joseph Smith unearthed a stone box buried in the Hill Cumorah near his family's home in Manchester, New York. The box contained an ancient record written on gold plates. He translated the record with the aid of seer stones, which he also unearthed, and published the translation as the Book of Mormon. © by Intellectual Reserve, Inc.

HISTORICAL ARCHAEOLOGY
AND THE LATTER-DAY SAINT PAST

The quest to discover the physical vestiges of the past lies at the center of all archaeology and helps explain the public's enduring fascination with the discipline. Who isn't thrilled with the idea of buried treasure from ages past? Members of The Church of Jesus Christ of Latter-day Saints are no different. In fact, beginning with the Church's founder, Joseph Smith, Latter-day Saints have long been fascinated with what can be accurately described as archaeological pursuits—the discovery of buried or concealed objects from ancient times and what they can reveal about the past.

It is this fundamental idea of revealing truth from the past, especially in connection with buried objects, that connects the history of The Church of Jesus Christ of Latter-day Saints with people's archaeological fascinations. Indeed, the very "keystone" of the religion—the Book of Mormon—was revealed from ancient gold plates that Joseph Smith unearthed from a stone box buried in a hillside in upstate New York (figure 1). With the gold plates were other relics from antiquity—"two stones in silver bows," which when "fastened to a breastplate, constituted what is called the Urim and Thummim," an ancient instrument used by "seers" of old (Joseph Smith—History 1:35; see also Mosiah 28:13–16). Joseph used the Urim and Thummim and another small "seer stone," which he had also discovered in the ground years before, in his translation of the Book of Mormon.[1]

The revealed text of the Book of Mormon itself further fuels the archaeological imagination by recounting other instances when ancient civilizations and objects were discovered. For example, it includes an account of an exploring party who inadvertently discovered the remnants of an earlier civilization. The record states they stumbled across "a land which was covered with bones of men, and of beasts, and was also covered with ruins of buildings of every kind." Among the detritus, they found twenty-four gold plates, as well as breastplates and swords (Mosiah 8:7–11; see also Ether 1:1–2).

The text of the Book of Mormon also mentions there would be three witnesses who would have the privilege of seeing the plates from which the book would be revealed (Ether 5:2–4; 2 Nephi 27:12). In June 1829, as Joseph Smith and his scribe, Oliver Cowdery, completed the manuscript for the Book of Mormon, Joseph received a revelation in which he learned that Oliver Cowdery and two other early supporters—David Whitmer and Martin Harris—would be the witnesses who would "have a view of the plates" and also of other ancient artifacts mentioned in the Book of Mormon, including "the breastplate, the sword of Laban, [and] the Urim and Thummim" (Doctrine and Covenants 17:1). A short while later, while engaged in prayer, an angel appeared to the men—first to Joseph, Oliver, and David and then to Joseph and Martin—showing them the engravings on the plates and the other ancient artifacts.[2] The written testimony of these three witnesses, in addition to the written testimony of eight other men to whom Joseph showed the ancient plates, has been published in every edition of the Book of Mormon since its first printing in 1830 and has further fired the archaeological fascination with the book and its origins.

Other key events in the history of the Church are likewise tied to the mythos of archaeology. Take for example the translation of the Latter-day Saint scripture known as the Book of Abraham and its ties to ancient Egyptian papyrus scrolls and mummies purchased by the Church in the summer of 1835 (figure 2). The fascination with these antiquities was captured by Oliver Cowdery, who wrote that the "mummies themselves are a curiosity and an astonishment, well calculated to arouse the mind to a reflection of past ages, when men strove, as at this day, to immortalize their names."[3] His fascination with the mummies was matched by his enthrallment with the papyri. Indeed, "for Cowdery and for Joseph Smith himself, the most potent connection with the past offered by the recently acquired antiquities lay in the papyri."[4]

FIGURE 2. One of ten surviving fragments of the Egyptian papyrus scrolls purchased by members of the Church in 1835. Joseph Smith used these scrolls during his translation of the Book of Abraham. © by Intellectual Reserve, Inc.

The previous summer, in June 1834, while Joseph Smith and other members of the Camp of Israel (Zion's Camp) journeyed across western Illinois on their way to Jackson County, Missouri, they dug into the top of a large mound and unearthed Native American skeletal remains and an associated projectile point.[5] Through vision, the Prophet learned that the skeletal remains were of a man named Zelph, a righteous warrior from Book of Mormon times, who was killed by the projectile point during a great battle.[6] Although such quasi-archaeological activities were common in the United States at this time, they would be considered unethical (and in some instances even illegal) today. Nonetheless, they clearly excited the archaeological imaginations of those who participated in 1834. That excitement continues today, as evidenced by the ongoing passionate debates about archaeological evidence for the Book of Mormon and its geography.[7]

Although Joseph Smith's experience with the Illinois burial mound led him to believe they were "wandering over the plains of the Nephites,"[8] his later encounters with published accounts of archaeological discoveries in

Mesoamerica inspired him to affirm that they also "support[ed] the testimony of the Book of Mormon."[9] In the end, as one scholar has asserted, "the thinking of the early church leaders regarding Book of Mormon geography was subject to modification, indicating that they themselves did not see the issue as settled."[10]

Despite the past (and present) uncertainty surrounding Book of Mormon archaeology and geography, many of the experiences early Church members had with ancient, buried objects was informed by a revelation dictated by Joseph Smith in December 1832 while living in Kirtland, Ohio. In this revelation the Lord commanded Church officers to establish "the school of the Prophets" (Doctrine and Covenants 88:127), in which those who held the priesthood were to "teach one another . . . diligently . . . in all things that pertain unto the kingdom of God" (vv. 77–78), in preparation for their mission to "testify and warn the people" (v. 81) of the imminent Second Coming and millennial reign of Jesus Christ (see vv. 87–117). Included in the list of those subjects "that [were] expedient for [them] to understand" were "things which *have been*" and, specifically, "things . . . *under the earth*" (Doctrine and Covenants 88:78–79; emphasis added). Given this context, early Church members' exposure to Egyptian mummies, Native American skeletal remains, and Mesoamerican ruins were to be understood in a broader metaphysical framework of "seek[ing] learning . . . by study and also by faith" (v. 118) in preparation for the time when "all people, both in heaven and earth" and even those "that are under the earth" (like Zelph) will receive the everlasting gospel and "give glory to him [the Lord Jesus Christ] who sitteth upon the throne, forever and ever" (vv. 103–4).

This same revelation also clarifies that a key component of the Saints' preparation was the establishment of "a house of God" (the Kirtland Temple), wherein the Saints would be taught and sanctified and to which the Lord would "come quickly, and receive [them] unto [Himself]" (vv. 119–26). Significantly, another revelation eight years later provided additional instructions about erecting another house of God—a temple in Nauvoo, Illinois—and again connected this cosmologically significant effort to the material remains of the ancient past. The revelation called upon all Saints to come to Nauvoo with, among other things, "all your antiquities; and with all who have knowledge of antiquities . . . and build a house . . . for the Most High to dwell therein . . . a place . . . [where] he may come to and restore again that which was lost unto you" (Doctrine and Covenants 124:25–28).[11]

These revelations as well as the Book of Mormon itself placed ancient material remains—be it an Egyptian mummy, Native American skeletal remains, or an antiquity for the Nauvoo temple—within a sacred cosmology. This framework is canonized in a revelation Joseph Smith received early in his prophetic ministry about the conditions and events preceding the Second Coming of Jesus Christ. In it the Lord declares: "And righteousness will I send down out of heaven; *and truth will I send forth out of the earth . . .*" (Moses 7:62; emphasis added). In this way, the various archaeological encounters of early Church members were more than mere intellectual curiosities. They were material evidence of the truths the Lord was revealing to them about His plan to redeem the earth and exalt all His children in the last days.

HISTORICAL ARCHAEOLOGY

Although archaeology is commonly associated with the ancient world, the material remains studied by archaeologists don't have to be thousands of years old. In fact, the branch of archaeology known as historical archaeology focuses on the more recent past—the last six hundred years of human history. Like all branches of archaeology, historical archeology relies on the material remains of the past to gain insights into human culture and history. But because of their focus on the more recent past, historical archaeologists also avail themselves of additional sources of historical information in their quest to understand the past. Chief among these is the documentary record of the past, which includes textual records like newspapers, diaries, and correspondence as well as historical paintings, photographs, maps, and other visual vestiges of the past. Historical archaeologists also look to oral histories of those who lived, or who knew of those who lived, in the time period and place of interest. Finally, in their pursuit of understanding the past, historical archaeologists can also gain insights from ethnography—the study of living peoples whose customs and practices are similar to those of the historical persons they are investigating.[12]

As a discipline, historical archaeology in the United States is relatively young. It emerged institutionally as part of the public works programs in the 1930s, when the US government sponsored excavations at notable historic sites like Jamestown, Virginia, to both create work for the unemployed and bolster national identity and morale during a time of economic crisis. Thirty years later, during another time of low morale and identity crisis in the United States, historical archaeology professionalized as an academic discipline, with the establishment of university curricula and the formation of distinct scholarly societies, organizations, and academic journals.[13] Today, historical archaeology is a thriving global discipline with ever-increasing numbers of practitioners and publications that are making meaningful contributions to our shared understanding of the recent past.[14] For example, the Society for Historical Archaeology, established in 1967, is now one of the largest archaeological organizations in the world.[15]

Even though historical archaeology is thriving as a discipline, throughout its relatively short history, historians and other archaeologists have frequently questioned its value to understanding the past. Unfortunately, disparagements continue in some circles even today. There are critics who view historical archaeology as merely a "handmaiden to history," capable of providing nothing but interesting footnotes to a past that is already known through the traditional historical record. Why sift through, they argue, the detritus of individuals and societies for whom we already have detailed records that describe, illustrate, and explain the past we are seeking to understand? They question what archaeology can possibly reveal of the recent past that we don't already know from history. Arguments such as these rest on the assumption that archaeology is best suited to study the ancient or nonliterate past with its material traces of clay and stone and not the recent past with its proliferation of written and visual sources of historical information.[16]

A closely related argument assumes that the material remains of the recent past have no real value to understanding history. Those that adopt this view have at times disparagingly referred to historical archaeology as "tin can archaeology," because they fail to see the intellectual value of what they perceive as nothing but modern trash. Archaeology's real subject matter, they argue, are the ancient material remains of long ago, not the familiar, everyday rubbish of the recent past.[17]

To counter these misperceptions, it is useful to consider the ways historical archaeology has contributed to our understanding of the recent past and, in particular, the Latter-day Saint past of the nineteenth and twentieth centuries. To do so, I will categorize the contributions into what I call the four *C's* of Historical Archaeology—confirm, complete, correct, and confuse. In sum, a historical archaeological approach can (1) *confirm* what we already know about the past, (2) *complete* our understanding of the past, (3) *correct* misperceptions about the past, or (4) *confuse* our interpretations of the past.

Below I will provide examples of how historical archaeological investigations have contributed to our understanding of the Latter-day Saint past in each of these four ways. At the outset, it is appropriate to acknowledge that these four categories are not mutually exclusive. Most historical archaeological investigations do more than one of these things at the same time. But for the sake of illustration, I will highlight specific aspects of otherwise multifaceted archaeology projects that demonstrate each of these ways that historical archaeology has contributed to our understanding of the Latter-day Saint past.

CONFIRM

The first, and perhaps most basic, contribution of historical archaeology to our understanding of the Latter-day Saint past is in providing confirmatory evidence of information known from other sources. Excavations sponsored by The Church of Jesus Christ of Latter-day Saints at many of its historic sites have performed this function. Take for example, the excavations at the Nauvoo Temple site in the 1960s.[18] Prior to any archaeological work at the site, the existence, size, general location, and appearance of the Nauvoo Temple was known from letters, journals, maps, drawings, and daguerreotypes (figure 3). Such preexisting historical knowledge, however, only heightened the thrill of discovery when a backhoe uncovered the first stone remains of the temple in Nauvoo in December 1962, confirming that physical remains of the historic temple still survived underground (figure

FIGURE 3. A daguerreotype of the Nauvoo Temple, circa 1846. On October 9, 1948, an arsonist's fire left only the temple's outer limestone walls intact. Less than two years later, a tornado toppled the temple's north wall and weakened the others. By 1853, only the temple's crumbling western facade remained standing. During the ensuing years, the ruins of the temple were completely dismantled by area residents, who salvaged some of the stones for use in other buildings. © by Intellectual Reserve, Inc.

FIGURE 4. Archaeologists uncovering the remains of the
Nauvoo Temple in 1969. © by Intellectual Reserve, Inc.

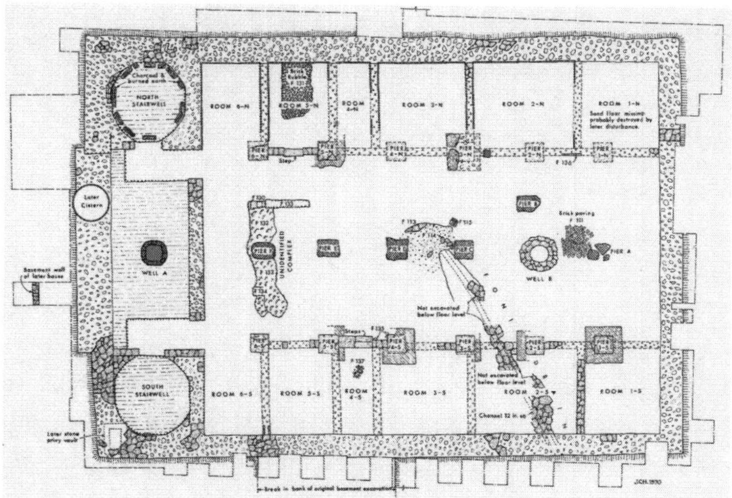

FIGURE 5. A drawing of the physical remains of the Nauvoo Temple as uncovered
through archaeological excavation. Originally published in Harrington and Harrington's *Rediscovery of the Nauvoo Temple: Report on Archeological Excavations*,
1971.

4). Further confirmation of the extensive surviving remains of the temple
emerged as teams of archaeologists continued to excavate the site over the
next seven years (figure 5).[19]

A more recent example of historical archaeology's role in confirming our understanding of the Latter-day past comes from investigations

FIGURE 6. The original Provo Tabernacle (left) and the city's second tabernacle (right), circa 1885. The interior of the second tabernacle was destroyed by fire in December 2010, which led to archaeological investigations of the first tabernacle, which had been razed in 1919. © by Intellectual Reserve, Inc.

conducted in 2011–2012 at the site of the original Provo Tabernacle.[20] When Provo's second tabernacle was tragically destroyed by fire in December 2010, few residents of the area remembered that an earlier tabernacle—one completed in the 1860s and razed fifty years later in 1919—once stood a short distance to the north in the same city block (figure 6). However, when leaders of The Church of Jesus Christ of Latter-day Saints announced the following year that the burned-out shell of the Provo Tabernacle would be restored and converted into a temple, staff from the historic sites division of the Church's History Department were quick to raise awareness of the earlier tabernacle, the location, size, design, and use of which was well documented in historic maps, photographs, and other records. Realizing that construction activities for the new temple would impact the site of the original tabernacle, employees of the Church History Department partnered with faculty and staff from Brigham Young University (BYU) to confirm whether anything of the earlier structure remained.

With help from BYU's Department of Geological Sciences, a three-dimensional (3D) ground-penetrating radar (GPR) survey was conducted in 2011. Like the radar used at airports to safely guide airplanes as they land, ground-penetrating radar utilizes an antenna which transmits electromagnetic signals into the earth. A computer attached to the antenna then records the "echoes" of those signals as they reflect off buried objects or surfaces whose electrical properties are substantially different than the surrounding soil. The speed at which the electromagnetic signals are reflected back to the antenna is used to estimate the depth of the buried objects and features. Thousands of signals are recorded every second as the antenna is moved across the ground along a series of closely spaced parallel and perpendicular transects that form a grid. Specialized software is then used to assemble the recorded information into a 3D volume of data that can be sliced and viewed at various depths or cross-sections. The ability of GPR to three-dimensionally visualize the subsurface of the earth is what makes it such a powerful tool for confirming the presence (or absence) of buried archaeological objects and features.[21]

The results of the GPR survey at the original Provo Tabernacle site clearly indicated the presence of subsurface features that closely corresponded with the shape and size of the structure known from maps and photographs (figure 7). A small test excavation by BYU's Office of Public Archaeology (OPA) exposed the southeast corner of a substantial stone foundation two feet underground, confirming that the GPR had indeed detected the buried remains of the original Provo Tabernacle.[22] Following this confirmation, the Church hired OPA to conduct a complete excavation of the site for the purpose of fully documenting the remains of the historic building before the area was impacted by the construction of the new temple. The fully excavated foundation of the original tabernacle further confirmed the footprint and layout of the early structure (figure 8).[23]

The confirmation of physical remains (or sometimes the absence thereof) is in many ways the most basic contribution of any archaeological excavation. It answers the fundamental question, "Does anything survive underground?" However, the role of historical archaeology to confirm what is already known about the past extends beyond this basic

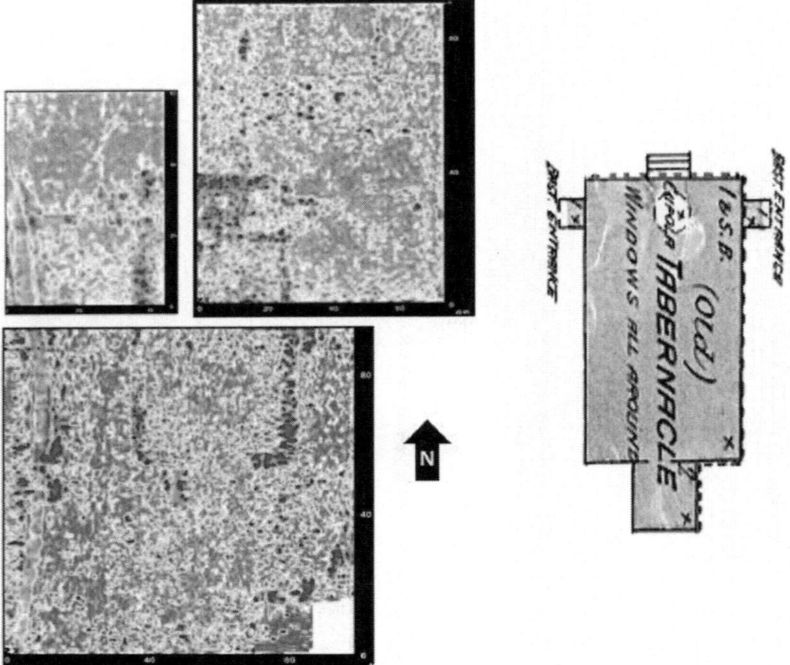

FIGURE 7. The results of a ground-penetrating radar survey at the site of the original Provo Tabernacle (left) closely corresponded with a drawing of the structure's footprint on an 1888 Sanborn fire insurance map (right).

question to also include material evidence that confirms our understanding of known past activities and behaviors at a particular site. The archaeological excavations of the original Provo Tabernacle are a case in point. In addition to confirming the original tabernacle's location, dimensions, and construction, the excavations revealed confirming evidence of many of the activities known to have taken place within the historic building. For example, a small advertisement on the front page of the November 14, 1908, issue of the *Utah County Democrat* documents that the Provo Sixth Ward hosted "famous chicken dinners" in the basement of the "old Provo meeting house" for an entire week. These were "all you can eat" events that cost only 25 cents per person. Excavations of the tabernacle's basement

FIGURE 8. The remains of the original Provo Tabernacle uncovered by archaeological excavation, 2012.

confirmed the use of this space for such activities. Not only did archaeologists uncover discarded chicken bones and fragments of ceramic dishes, which were presumably used in community meals such as the one advertised in the newspaper, they also recovered several coins, some of which possibly fell through the cracks between the tabernacle's floorboards as people paid for the 25-cent all-you-can-eat chicken dinners.[24]

The same is true for other artifacts uncovered during the excavations of the tabernacle's basement. For example, the numerous fragments of slate pencils and writing tablets recovered by archaeologists confirm the use of the building's basement for school-related activities (figure 9). Not only did an early elementary school meet there for a time, but students and teachers of the Brigham Young Academy also temporarily used the space after the building they had been using burned down. The discovery of a few small toys further confirms the presence of children in the space. Although it's possible the children's toys could have been lost during activities like all-you-can-eat chicken dinners in the tabernacle's basement, it

FIGURE 9. Children's toys and slate pencils uncovered during the excavations of the original Provo Tabernacle. The presence of artifacts like these helps to confirm that the building's basement was used as a classroom for schoolchildren.

is just as likely (if not more so) that such small toys were lost during times when the space was being used as a classroom for schoolchildren.[25]

COMPLETE

If the only way historical archaeology contributed to our understanding of the past was to confirm what is known from other sources, then perhaps the critics who claim it is nothing but a handmaiden to history would be justified in their criticisms. Fortunately, historical archaeology's contributions go beyond mere confirmation; it can, and often does, contribute new information about the past and therefore helps *complete* our understanding of the places, people, and events of earlier times.

The 1960s excavations of the Nauvoo Temple illustrate historical archaeology's ability to help complete our understanding of the past. Although it was already known from other sources that the Latter-day Saints had constructed first a wooden and later a stone baptismal font in the basement of the temple, it was only through the archaeological excavations that important details came to light of what that ritual space looked

FIGURE 10. A section of the original brick floor of the Nauvoo Temple's basement, adjacent to the 1840s well that was used to fill the temple's baptismal font. © by Intellectual Reserve, Inc.

like and how it functioned. For example, near the east end of the temple's basement, archaeologists uncovered an area of bricks arranged in a herringbone pattern (figure 10).[26] This previously unknown fact, that the temple's basement had an intricately laid brick floor, was later incorporated into the reconstruction of the Nauvoo Temple over 150 years after the original brick floor was built. Adjacent to the area of brick flooring, archaeologists also uncovered a deep well that the 1840s builders of the temple had dug and lined with shaped stone.[27] The well's proximity to where the baptismal font once sat facilitated filling the font with water. Finally, underneath what would have been the temple's basement floor, archaeologists also discovered the remains of a stone-lined drain, which conveyed the water from the baptismal font to an area outside the walls of the temple.[28] Details like these, known only through archaeology, have helped complete our understanding of the appearance and function of the original temple's basement.

Additional important discoveries were made during the excavations of the temple site. While exploring the area where the baptismal font once sat, archaeologists uncovered a linear alignment of stone piers constructed at even intervals along the centerline of the temple's basement. Upon closer examination, they discovered that some of these piers were built from salvaged stones from the baptismal font, which helped them determine that the piers were built by a group of French Icarians in the late 1840s. Before the excavations, the history of the Icarians' attempts to rebuild the interior of the temple, which had been destroyed by fire in 1848, was well known. But *how* they attempted to do this was not known. The discovery and analysis of the stone piers contributed new information about the ways the Icarians reused the remains of the burned-out temple in their efforts to engineer and construct a new floor for the building. Sadly, their efforts were abandoned once a tornado toppled the northern wall of the temple in 1850. Nevertheless, the stone piers survived, and their discovery during the archaeological excavations in the 1960s helped complete our understanding of this part of the temple's story.[29]

Another example of how historical archaeology has helped complete our understanding of the past comes from the excavations of the original Provo Tabernacle. Little is known about the appearance of the original tabernacle's interior. Surviving architectural drawings indicate the location of the columns that supported a balcony, the arrangement of the seating, the placement of the speaker's stand, and even the position of heating stoves on the main floor of the building.[30] But no known photographs of the tabernacle's interior survive. In his prayer to dedicate the building on August 24, 1867, Apostle John Taylor blessed, among many other things, the structure's plastered walls, providing additional clues about what the inside of the tabernacle might have looked like.[31] But it wasn't until archaeologists started excavating the site that important details of the tabernacle's interior began to emerge. Most notably, the archaeologists uncovered numerous fragments of wall plaster, many of which were painted in vibrant shades of red, yellow, brown, tan, purple, and blue (figure 11). In addition, the excavations revealed sections of intricate decorative plaster

FIGURE 11. Fragments of colorfully painted wall plaster (left) and decorative plaster moldings (right) uncovered during excavations of the original Provo Tabernacle.

moldings made by skilled craftsmen and similarly painted in bright hues to adorn the structure's interior.[32] Taken together, these archaeological discoveries reveal that the interior of the tabernacle must have been a colorful and elaborately decorated space. Although we may never know exactly what the inside of the original Provo Tabernacle looked like, the archaeological excavations of the site have contributed to a more complete understanding of this significant structure's interior.

When it comes to completing our understanding of the past, historical archaeology's contributions extend beyond construction details of old buildings. It can also complete our understanding of past human behaviors and cultural values. A good example of this comes from the archaeological investigations at Iosepa, a settlement in Skull Valley, Utah, inhabited by Pacific Islander (mostly Hawai'ian) converts to The Church of Jesus Christ of Latter-day Saints from 1889 to 1917 (figure 12). Much is known about Iosepa from existing documentary sources.[33] There are surviving photographs of some of the town's residents and their homes (figure 13). There are federal census records from 1900 and 1910 that list the names, ages, and occupations of most of the individuals living in the town at those times. There are also numerous newspaper articles that document various events and happenings over the years. A plat map of the town, created in 1908, shows the size and arrangement of the town blocks, lots, and streets, all of which were patterned after Joseph Smith's plat for the City of Zion. Iosepa's plat map also reveals how the town's residents assigned cultural meaning to

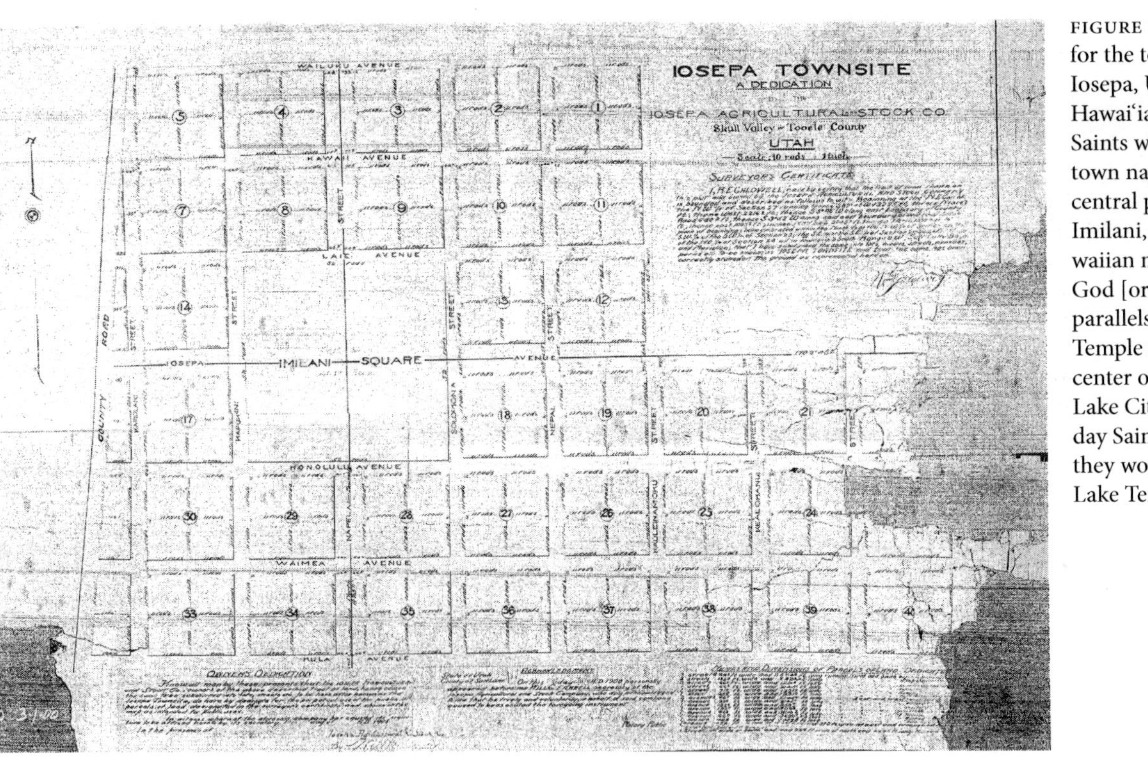

FIGURE 12. Plat map for the townsite of Iosepa, Utah, 1908. The Hawai'ian Latter-day Saints who occupied the town named their large central public square Imilani, which in Hawaiian means "to seek God [or heaven]." This parallels the purpose of Temple Square at the center of nearby Salt Lake City, where Latter-day Saints seek God as they worship in the Salt Lake Temple.

FIGURE 13. Some of the over two hundred residents of Iosepa, Utah, 1913. Courtesy of the Utah State Historical Society.

their public spaces by naming the streets and avenues after significant places from the Hawai'ian Islands and important persons in the Pacific Islander community.[34] There is even a small cemetery at the town site, where several engraved headstones survive. Yet, despite all that is known from these and other sources of information, there is still a great deal we can learn through historical archaeological research to complete our knowledge and understanding of what life was like for those who lived at Iosepa.

Take, for example, what has been learned through historical archaeological research about the family of John and Emily Mahoe. John K. N. Mahoe moved to Iosepa in 1889 with his first wife, Hannah Auld. Hannah passed away from Hansen's disease (leprosy) and is buried in the Iosepa cemetery. John remarried, to Emily Umi in 1898, and they had fourteen children, twelve in Iosepa and two after returning to Hawai'i in 1917. Archaeological investigations of their homesite identified and uncovered one of the family's privies, which had been filled with many of their household and personal items. An analysis of these artifacts suggest they had been thrown away around the same time the Mahoes and most of the other residents of Iosepa moved to Hawai'i at the invitation of the president of the Church in 1917. In addition to numerous glass containers and large quantities of food remains and personal items, the Mahoe's privy

FIGURE 14. Examples of the plain and inexpensive whiteware plates (left) and the decorated, more expensive teacups and saucers (right) discovered during excavations of a privy on the lot where the Mahoe family lived in Iosepa.

contained the remains of at least 63 ceramic vessels, represented by 257 individual ceramic fragments. When considered as a whole, this collection of ceramics reveals a significant pattern. All the tablewares are plain whiteware plates or deep soup bowls, while the great majority of the non-tableware forms (i.e., mainly teacups and saucers) are either decorated whitewares or porcelains (figure 14). This dichotomy, between plain, inexpensive tablewares and more elaborately decorated and more expensive teaware and related special forms, offers insight into some of the Mahoe family's social negotiations at Iosepa.[35]

Historical archaeologists studying Euro-American sites have argued that differences in the decoration between these two categories of ceramics (tableware and teaware) suggest that the people who used them placed different social meanings on the activities they represent (household meals vs. social "teas").[36] For Euro-Americans, social teas were traditionally the arena in which people communicated their household status to others in the community. But meals were primarily activities in which only members of the household participated. When viewed from this perspective, the stark difference between the Mahoe's plain, inexpensive tableware and their more expensive decorated teaware might suggest that they were participating in a form of conspicuous consumption or social display of status or prestige by investing more of their resources on ceramics that would be publicly displayed, while maintaining rather modest ceramics for their more private dinner table.

Ethnographers of twentieth-century Hawai'ians, however, have documented the paramount emphasis on affiliative values in Hawai'ian culture and the "devaluation of behavior oriented toward raising one's prestige vis-à-vis others."[37] In this light, "resources are seen as a *means* to maintaining and expanding interpersonal networks rather than as an *end* in themselves."[38] Contributing to this emphasis on interpersonal ties is the strong stigma attached to behaviors that elevate one above his or her peers: "To make a public bid for recognition by flaunting one's successes is considered to be extremely bad taste and is a sure path to public ostracism."[39] One ethnographer's informants frequently conveyed this sentiment by saying, "We are like crabs in a basket. As soon as one begins to crawl out the others reach up to pull him back."[40] This is not to say that kinship ranking, which is usually determined by age, is not important in Hawai'ian family groupings—for it is. But outside of the family, "egalitarian pressures are very strong between nonkinsmen and informal sanctions are brought to bear on those who flaunt their achievements or who seek public recognition."[41] It is also clear that the "avoidance of showing off extends to such lifestyle features as housing and furnishings, thereby reducing incentive to accumulate for display and recognition." In the same vein, however, "restrictions on consumption do not extend . . . to items which are seen as facilitating interpersonal relations and hospitality."[42] Thus, insofar as teaware items could be essential tools in the establishment and maintenance of important social relationships, the Mahoe's more expensive decorated teaware, as opposed to their less-expensive plain white tableware, should not be viewed as a blatant display of status or prestige but as one way they emphasized the value they placed on interpersonal relations.[43]

In the case of Iosepa, historical archaeology has helped complete our understanding of this unique Latter-day Saint settlement and its Pacific

Islander residents. A careful analysis of the ceramics found in an abandoned privy has revealed attitudes and behaviors of the Mahoe family
that were not known from other sources. We not only know what kinds of
dishes they were able to purchase and use while living in Iosepa but also
how they used them in ways that reflect the specific cultural values and
attitudes they held towards their family and community.

CORRECT

Another important way that historical archaeology contributes to our
shared understanding of history is by correcting what we think we already
know about the past. Such has been the case with the historical archaeology at the Peter and Mary Whitmer Farm in Fayette, New York. The
Whitmer Farm is where Joseph Smith and his early followers formally
organized a branch of the Church of Christ[44] in April 1830. It is also where
Joseph Smith completed the translation of the Book of Mormon from the
ancient gold plates with which he was entrusted. The Whitmer Farm was
also the place where an angel showed those gold plates to three others,
who became witnesses of their reality and of the divine power with which
Joseph had translated them.[45]

Given the significance of these and other events in Latter-day Saint
history, the Whitmer Farm has been a place of importance to the Church
and its members for many years. Prior to the Church's purchase of the
hundred-acre farm in 1926, various interested individuals visited the site,
wanting to identify the location of the log farmhouse in which the significant historical events occurred. These visitors encountered a farm whose
buildings and landscapes had changed since the Whitmer family lived
there in the early nineteenth century. This resulted in considerable confusion and debate about the location of the original log home, which in turn
spurred intensive research efforts by Church-affiliated historians, who
scoured archives, collected oral histories, and examined existing structures until they felt confident in their conclusions.[46]

In 1969, these historians asked Dale Berge, a historical archaeologist
at Brigham Young University, to excavate the site where they believed the
Whitmer log home originally stood (figure 15). The excavations revealed
a concentration of nineteenth- and twentieth-century artifacts distributed

FIGURE 15. Dr. Dale Berge (right) with two students, Bill Johnson and John Call, excavating the site where historians believed the log home, in which a branch of the Church of Christ was organized, was located on the Peter and Mary Whitmer Farm in Fayette New York (1969).

in an area approximately 30 by 40 feet in size. In his published report of the excavations, Berge noted that "most of the artifacts . . . were so fragmented that only a very general time range [for the site] could be established." He also indicated a "problem which cannot be answered: If the [Whitmer] log house was torn down before 1888, why do artifacts dating to after this date appear at the site?"[47] Despite these challenges, researchers accepted the results of the excavation as confirmation of the location of the original Whitmer log home. Ten years after the archaeological investigation, workers built and furnished a log cabin on the site that Berge had excavated, using materials reclaimed from other old log structures in the area (figure 16). They also built a large meetinghouse and visitors' center a short distance to the east to commemorate the growth of the Church since its beginnings in 1830. On April 6, 1980, exactly 150 years after Joseph Smith and his followers formally organized the Church, the newly built Whitmer log home was dedicated by the president of the Church and opened to the public as an official Church historic site.[48]

FIGURE 16. The log home constructed by The Church of Jesus Christ of Latter-day Saints in 1979 to commemorate the bicentennial anniversary of the Church's organization. The replica home was built on the site excavated by Dale Berge ten years earlier. Courtesy of The Church of Jesus Christ of Latter-day Saints.

The assumed location of the Whitmer's original farmhouse has become cemented in the public consciousness as tens of thousands of people tour the replica log home each year. Recently, however, the research on which the location of the reconstructed log home was based is being reevaluated in light of new archaeological discoveries that demonstrate the ability of historical archaeology to correct our understanding of the past.

The first archaeological clues that hinted at an alternate location for the original Whitmer log home emerged in the spring of 2002. At that time, missionaries assigned to give tours of the Church's historic site discovered various pieces of broken glass, ceramics, and bricks while walking over recently plowed fields southwest of the replica log home. Those artifacts were sent to the Church History Department in Salt Lake City, where they were properly cataloged and stored but not given much attention until 2018 when researchers initiated additional studies of the Whitmer Farm historic site. Upon closer examination, the artifacts were determined to be from the early nineteenth century, the time period associated with

FIGURE 17. Archaeological excavations at the Peter and Mary Whitmer Farm, 2022.

the Whitmer family's occupation of the farm. This discovery led to an archaeological survey of the entire hundred-acre farm, including the area immediately surrounding the replica log home, where it was assumed the Whitmer family had lived.[49]

The survey results were both surprising and enlightening. The only location on the entire hundred-acre property where early nineteenth-century artifacts were abundantly found was the same field where the missionaries had discovered artifacts in 2002. When plotted on a map of the farm's boundaries, this singular location is situated in the middle of the property, a few hundred feet off the main road. This is significant because it corresponds to a known pattern of building among Pennsylvania Germans, the ethnic group to which the Whitmers belonged. Unlike their English-descended counterparts, who typically built their homes close to roads, families of Pennsylvania German descent like the Whitmers preferred to build their homesteads some distance away from the main roads.[50]

Knowing that this area was the only place on the hundred-acre farm where substantial artifacts from the right time period were located, researchers conducted additional, more extensive, archaeological investigation at the site (figure 17).[51] Systematic test pits followed by larger excavation areas recovered a sizable collection of Whitmer-period artifacts. The majority of the artifacts can be classified into two major groupings—domestic and architectural. Many are small fragments of ceramics that were typically used in domestic settings, while others are architectural in nature, including various brick fragments. When

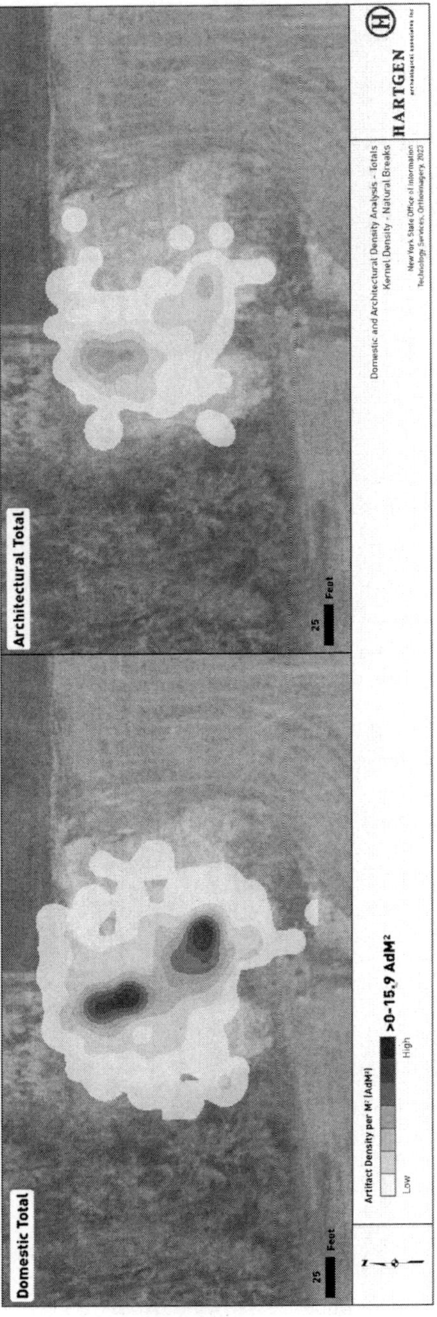

FIGURE 18. Map showing clusters of artifact densities at the Whitmer Farm that suggest the location of areas where the Whitmer family lived and worked.

the locations of these artifacts are plotted on a map, significant patterns emerge revealing distinct clusters that likely represent activity areas from the time the Whitmer family lived on the farm (figure 18).

Evidence of multiple activity areas is not surprising given the demographics of the Whitmer family and their agricultural lifestyle. An early nineteenth-century farm like theirs would necessarily require various kinds of buildings to support their farming activities and their expanding family. In 1830, the year before they sold the farm and moved to Ohio, the federal census indicates three "heads of families" on the farm—Peter Sr., the patriarch of the family, and his two oldest sons, Jacob and Christian, who had married by this time.[52] Although the married sons could have continued to reside under the same roof as their parents, it is just as likely that one or both would have lived in modest homes of their own. This could account for the artifactual evidence pointing to multiple activity areas on the farm.

It is hoped that additional historical archaeological research will help create a more accurate understanding of the Whitmer Farm historic site by revealing further insights about the locations of structures and other features, as well as clues about the Whitmer family's lifestyle during the time they lived on the farm. What has been learned to date demonstrates the way historical archaeology can correct erroneous assumptions and misinterpretations of the past. Whereas previous generations of researchers did their best with the information available to them at the time, current research at the Whitmer Farm is rewriting what we thought we knew about the farm and its layout. In this way, historical archaeology is significantly contributing to a more accurate understanding of the past.

CONFUSE

Even when historical archaeology confirms, completes, and corrects our knowledge of the past, there are times when it can also confuse. Such was the case with the archaeological investigation of the burial grounds at Far West, the short-lived nineteenth-century Latter-day Saint settlement in northwest Missouri. By the time historical archaeology was employed to investigate the site, historians had already published a good deal of information about the historic burial grounds.[53] The site is believed to contain the graves of approximately sixty-five individuals.[54] After the Latter-day Saints left Far West in 1839, the burial grounds were abandoned and the grave markers either deteriorated or were removed over the course of time. A fence surrounded the burial grounds as late as the 1890s, but by the turn of the twentieth century, most of the site had been converted to plowed farmland. Before all physical evidence of the burial grounds was obliterated, however, eyewitnesses provided general descriptions of the site, including directions and distances from the location at the center of the Far West settlement where the Latter-day Saints had planned to build a temple. Although land records and plat maps generally confirm the information from eyewitnesses, they are not sufficient to pinpoint the precise location of the burial grounds with absolute certainty. Hence, researchers turned to various archaeological methods to try to positively identify the site of the historic burial grounds.

The first method utilized was a survey by historic human remains detection dogs. These dogs, which, as their name suggests, are specially trained to detect the scent of historic human remains, have successfully identified historic graves in similarly unmarked cemeteries.[55] At the Far West Burial Grounds site, a total of five dogs were used to survey a thirty-one-acre area. The results of the survey indicated that the scent of human remains was confined to an approximately two-acre area in the northwest corner of the search area. Significantly, this area of scent concentration corresponds with information gleaned from other historical sources, including a statement from a woman who recalled passing an abandoned cemetery on her way to school and an 1897 plat map that shows an unlabeled rectangular feature immediately west of the schoolhouse where the woman attended school as a child (figure 19).[56]

Following the dog search, the smaller two-acre area of interest was surveyed using more precise archaeological instruments, including ground-penetrating radar and magnetometry, to locate actual grave plots. Although both surveys successfully visualized the buried remains of the schoolhouse that once sat on the northwest corner of the site, neither instrument detected any graves. Puzzled by these results, the archaeologists resorted to traditional excavation techniques to try and uncover

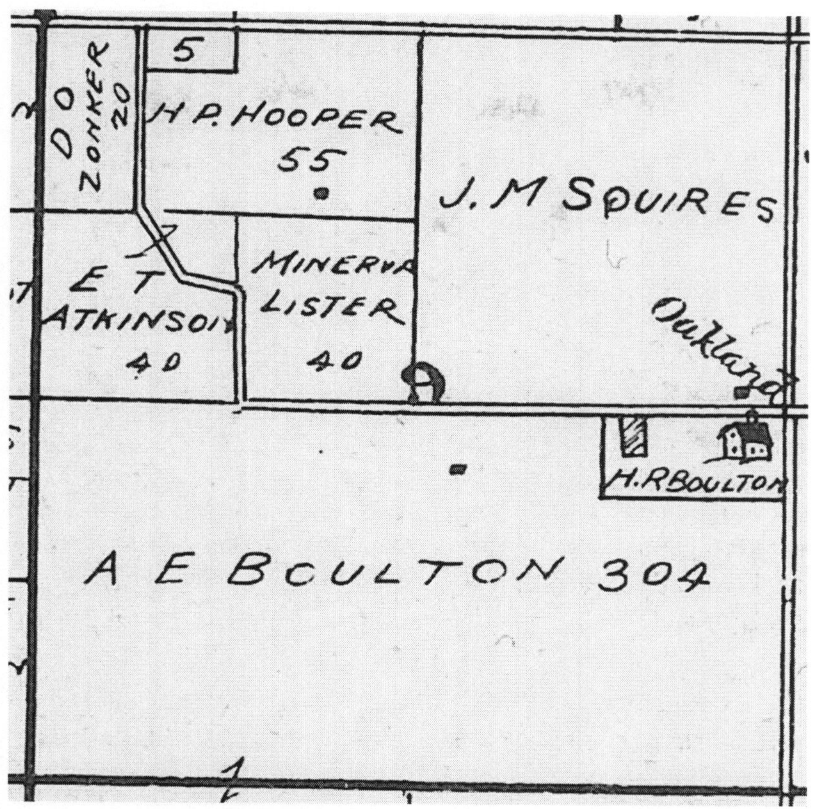

FIGURE 19. 1897 plat map showing an unmarked rectangular feature immediately west of the Oakland Schoolhouse. Although it is unknown if the rectangle represents the Far West Burial Grounds, its location west of the schoolhouse is consistent with statements given by eyewitnesses.

any evidence of the suspected graves in the search area. Using a backhoe, they excavated six trenches across those areas of the site where the dogs had detected human remains scent (figure 20). Remarkably, not a single artifact or any other indication of a grave was found. Befuddled by the absence of physical evidence, the archaeologists backfilled the trenches and abandoned the search for the graves.[57]

In this instance, historical archaeology has resulted in more confusion than confirmation. Even though historical documentation and the dog survey all pointed to the northwest corner of the search area as

FIGURE 20. Trenches excavated by historical archaeologists at the presumed location of the Far West Burial Grounds in 2013. In spite of historical and other data that pointed to the suspected location of the historic cemetery, no physical evidence of graves was discovered during intensive archaeological investigations at the site.

the location of the Far West Burial Grounds, archaeologists did not discover any tangible evidence of the approximately sixty-five historic graves despite utilizing several robust techniques in their investigation. Although there may be a rational explanation for these confusing results, to date there remain more questions than answers. It is often in such confusion, however, that new insights and awareness emerge. As historical archaeologists grapple with the seemingly unexplainable, they are forced to consider new approaches and interpretations that can ultimately lead to new knowledge and ways of understanding the past. Perhaps someday the location of the graves in the Far West Burial Grounds will be known. But until then The Church of Jesus Christ of Latter-day Saints will preserve and maintain the site in hopes that new technologies or information will emerge and lead to new evidence that will confirm, complete, or correct our understanding of the historic cemetery.

CONCLUSION

The potential of historical archaeology to significantly contribute to our understanding of the Latter-day Saint past is virtually limitless. There are innumerable opportunities for historical archaeologists to confirm, complete, and correct what we already know about Latter-day Saint history. There will no doubt be instances where efforts result in confusion, but it is often in those situations where historical archaeology can make its greatest contributions.

NOTES

1   The Church of Jesus Christ of Latter-day Saints, "Book of Mormon Translation," Church History Topics, accessed December 8, 2024, https://www.churchofjesuschrist.org/study/history/topics/book-of-mormon-translation.

2   W. H. Kelley, "Letter from Elder W. H. Kelley," *The Saints' Herald*, March 1, 1882, 68. See also *The Standard of Truth, 1815–1846*, vol. 1 of *Saints: The Story of the Church of Jesus Christ in the Latter Days* (Salt Lake City, UT: The Church of Jesus Christ of Latter-day Saints, 2018), 73–74.

3   Oliver Cowdery to William Frye, December 25, 1835, in Cowdery, Letterbook, 1833–1838, 75. Huntington Library, San Marino, CA. Cited in "Book of Abraham and Related Manuscripts," *Joseph Smith Papers*, https://www.josephsmithpapers.org/intro/introduction-to-revelations-and-translations-volume-4.

4   Robin Scott Jensen and Brian M. Hauglid, eds., "Introduction," in *Revelations and Translations*, vol. 4: *Book of Abraham and Related Manuscripts*, facsimile edition, vol. 4 of the Revelations and Translations series of *The Joseph Smith Papers*, ed. Ronald K. Esplin, Matthew J. Grow, Matthew C. Godfrey, and R. Eric Smith (Salt Lake City: Church Historian's Press, 2018); see also "Book of Abraham Translation," Church History Topics, accessed December 26, 2024, https://www.churchofjesuschrist.org/study/history/topics/book-of-abraham-translation; "Translation and Historicity of the Book of Abraham," Gospel Topics Essays, accessed December 26, 2024, https://www.churchofjesuschrist.org/study/manual/gospel-topics-essays/translation-and-historicity-of-the-book-of-abraham.

5   More recent archaeological investigations of this mound—now known as Naples-Russell Mound #8—have revealed that it is a Hopewell burial mound of the early Middle Woodland period (ca. 50 BC to AD 100). See Kenneth B. Farnsworth, "Lamanitish Arrows and Eagles with Lead Eyes: Tales of the First Recorded Explorations in an Illinois Valley Hopewell Mound," *Illinois Archaeology* 22, no. 1 (2010): 25–48.

6   Donald Q. Cannon, "Zelph Revisited," in *Regional Studies in the Latter-day Saint Church History: Illinois*, ed. H. Dean Garret (Provo, UT: Department of Church History and Doctrine, Brigham Young University, 1995), 57–109; Kenneth W. Godfrey, "The Zelph Story," *BYU Studies* 29, no. 2 (1989): 31–56; Kenneth W. Godfrey, "What Is the Significance

of Zelph in the Study of Book of Mormon Geography?" *Journal of Book of Mormon Studies* 8, no. 2 (1999): 70–79; Thomas J. Riley, "Joseph Smith, Zelph's Mound, and the Armies of Zion: The Construction of American Indians from Archaeological Evidence in Illinois in the Nineteenth Century," *Illinois Archaeology* 55, no. 1–2 (1993): 24–32.

7   The purpose of this article is not to contribute to, or give a detailed history of, the debates about archaeological evidence of the Book of Mormon or its geography. For a history and overview of these debates, see, Bruce R. Dahl, "Mormons and American Archaeology: A Brief History" (MA Thesis, California State University Northridge, 1994), and Andrew H. Hedges, "Book of Mormon Geographies," *BYU Studies Quarterly* 60, no. 3 (2021): 193–202.

8   Joseph Smith to Emma Smith, 4 June 1834, p. 57, The Joseph Smith Papers, https://www .josephsmithpapers.org/paper-summary/letter-to-emma-smith-4-june-1834/2.

9   Joseph Smith to John M. Bernhisel, 16 November 1841, p. 1, The Joseph Smith Papers, https://www.josephsmithpapers.org/paper-summary/letter-to-johnm-bernhisel -16november-1841/1.

10   Godfrey, "What Is the Significance of Zelph," 76.

11   This same revelation informed plans to establish a museum of antiquities and other "curiosities" in Nauvoo. See Glen Leonard, "Antiquities, Curiosities, and Latter-day Saint Museums," in *The Disciple as Witness: Essays on Latter-day Saint History and Doctrine in Honor of Richard Lloyd Anderson*, ed. Stephen D. Ricks, Donald W. Parry, and Andrew H. Hedges (Provo, UT: Foundation for Ancient Research and Mormon Studies, 2000), 291–325.

12   Charles E. Orser Jr., *Historical Archaeology* (New York: Routledge, 2017).

13   Benjamin C. Pykles, "A Brief History of Historical Archaeology in the United States," *SAA Archaeological Record* 8, no. 3 (May 2008): 32–34; Jim Ayres, "Early Classes in Historical Archaeology," *SAA Archaeological Record* 8, no. 4 (September 2008): 3.

14   David Gaimster and Teresita Majewski, eds., *International Handbook of Historical Archaeology* (New York: Springer, 2009); Dan Hicks and Mary C. Beaudry, eds., *The Cambridge Companion to Historical Archaeology* (Cambridge: Cambridge University Press, 2006).

15   Society for Historical Archaeology, "Who We Are," accessed March 4, 2023, https://sha .org/about-us.

16   Barbara J. Little, *Historical Archaeology: Why the Past Matters* (London and New York: Routledge, 2016).

17   David T. Yoder, "Interpreting the 50-Year Rule: How a Simple Phrase Leads to a Complex Problem," *Advances in Archaeological Practice* 2, no. 4 (November 2014): 324–37.

18   Virginia S. Harrington and J. C. Harrington, *Rediscovery of the Nauvoo Temple: Report on Archaeological Excavations* (Salt Lake City, UT: Nauvoo Restoration, 1971).

19   Benjamin C. Pykles, *Excavating Nauvoo: The Mormons and the Rise of Historical Archaeology in America* (Lincoln: University of Nebraska Press, 2010), 198–212, 251–56.

20   Ryan W. Saltzgiver, "'Ye People of Provo, Build That House': The Original Provo Tabernacle and the Building of a City in Zion," *Utah Archaeology* 27, no. 1 (2014): 111–48.

21   Lawrence B. Conyers, *Ground-Penetrating Radar for Archaeology* (Walnut Creek, CA: AltaMira Press, 2004), 149–59.

22   John H. McBride, Benjamin C. Pykles, Emily Utt, and R. William Keach II,

"Rediscovering Provo's First Tabernacle with Ground Penetrating Radar," *BYU Studies Quarterly* 51, no. 2 (2012): 61–77.

23   Deborah C. Harris, "The Original Provo Tabernacle: Report on the Archaeological Excavations" (Office of Public Archaeology Technical Series No. 14-2, Brigham Young University, 2016).

24   Ryan W. Saltzgiver, "Prototype for Zion: The Original Provo Tabernacle and the Construction of Mormon Zion in the American West" (MA thesis, Brigham Young University, 2015), 125–29, 147–48.

25   Saltzgiver, "Prototype for Zion," 153–55.

26   Harrington and Harrington, *Rediscovery of the Nauvoo Temple*, 23–28.

27   Harrington and Harrington, *Rediscovery of the Nauvoo Temple*, 29. See also Pykles, *Excavating Nauvoo*, 252.

28   Harrington and Harrington, *Rediscovery of the Nauvoo Temple*, 40–41.

29   Harrington and Harrington, *Rediscovery of the Nauvoo Temple*, 10–11. See also Dee F. Green and Larry Bowles, "Excavation of the Mormon Temple Remains at Nauvoo, Illinois: First Season," *Florida Anthropologist* 17, no. 2 (1964), 78–79.

30   Truman O. Angell architectural drawings, 1851–1867; in Unidentified Drawings, undated; Plan for a meetinghouse; Church History Library, accessed December 26, 2024, https://catalog.churchofjesuschrist.org/assets/792ca054-6878-4353-8635 -67baca59fa51/0/0?lang=eng.

31   La Verl Christensen, *Provo's Two Tabernacles and the People Who Built Them* (Provo Utah East Stake, 1983), 70.

32   Harris, "Original Provo Tabernacle," 38, 69–70, 114; Saltzgiver, " 'Ye People of Provo,' " 135; Ryan W. Saltzgiver, "Prototype for Zion," 110–13.

33   Matthew Kester, *Remembering Iosepa: History, Place, and Religion in the American West* (Oxford: Oxford University Press, 2013); Dennis H. Atkin, "A History of Iosepa, the Utah Polynesian Colony" (MA thesis, Brigham Young University, 1958); Tracey E. Panek, "Life at Iosepa, Utah's Polynesian Colony," *Utah Historical Quarterly* 60, no. 1 (Winter 1992): 64–77; Leonard J. Arrington, "The L.D.S. Hawaiian Colony at Skull Valley," *Improvement Era*, May 1954, 314–15, 365–67.

34   Benjamin C. Pykles and Jonathan S. Reeves, "Hawaiian Latter-day Saints in the Utah Desert: The Negotiation of Identity at Iosepa," *Historical Archaeology* 55 (2021): 501–10.

35   Benjamin C. Pykles, "The Negotiation of Cultural Identity in the Mormon Domain: A View from Iosepa, Utah's Pacific Islander Latter-day Saint Settlement," unpublished manuscript in the author's possession.

36   Diana diZerega Wall, "The Ritualization of Family Dinner in New York City" (paper presented at the First Joint Archaeological Congress, Baltimore, MD, 1989).

37   Alan Howard, "Households, Families and Friends in a Hawaiian-American Community" (Working Papers of the East-West Population Institute, no. 19, East-West Center, Honolulu, Hawai'i, 1971), 4.

38   Alan Howard, *Ain't No Big Thing: Coping Strategies in a Hawaiian-American Community* (Honolulu: The University Press of Hawaii, 1974), 26.

39   Howard, *Ain't No Big Thing*, 26.

40   Howard, "Households, Families and Friends," 4.

41   Howard, "Households, Families and Friends," 4.

42   Howard, *Ain't No Big Thing*, 26–27.

43   Pykles, "Negotiation of Cultural Identity."

44   It was not until 1838 when the current name of the Church—The Church of Jesus Christ of Latter-day Saints—was adopted. See Doctrine and Covenants section 115.

45   Larry C. Porter, "The Peter Whitmer Log Home: Cradle of Mormonism," *Religious Educator* 12, no. 3 (2011): 177–88.

46   Porter, "Peter Whitmer Log Home," 189–94.

47   Dale L. Berge, "Archaeology at the Peter Whitmer Farm, Seneca County, New York," *BYU Studies* 13, no. 2 (1973): 198, 200.

48   Porter, "Peter Whitmer Log Home," 194–97.

49   Powers Archaeology LLC, "Phase I (IA and IB) Cultural Resource Investigations for the Properties Associated with the Peter and Mary Whitmer Historic Site, Town of Fayette, Seneca County, New York" (report on file at the Church History Library, Salt Lake City, Utah, December 31, 2019).

50   John T. Humphrey, "Mid-Eighteenth-Century Life of Rural Pennsylvania Germans," *Pennsylvania Mennonite Heritage*, October 2000, 17; Gabrielle Lanier, "Landscapes," in *Architecture and Landscape of the Pennsylvania Germans, 1720–1920*, ed. Sally McMurry and Nancy Van Dolsen (Philadelphia: University of Pennsylvania Press, 2011), 13.

51   Hartgen Archeological Associates, Inc., "Archeological Investigation 2020 Season: Whitmer Farm, Church of Jesus Christ of Latter-day Saints" (report on file at the Church History Library, Salt Lake City, Utah, January 2022).

52   1830 United States census, Fayette, Seneca County, New York.

53   Michael S. Riggs and Alexander L. Baugh, "'That They Might Rest Where the Ashes of the Latter-day Saints Reposed': The Far West, Missouri, Burial Ground," *Mormon Historical Studies* 9, no. 1 (Spring 2008): 135–42.

54   Janet Lisonbee and Annette Curtis, *Missouri Mormon Burials: Obituaries and Life Sketches of the Early Saints Who Died and Are Buried in Missouri* (Independence: Missouri Mormon Frontier Foundation, 2008), 40–60.

55   Carey L. Baxter and Michael L. Hargrave, *Guidance on the Use of Historic Human Remains Detection Dogs for Locating Unmarked Cemeteries*, Department of Defense Legacy Resource Management Program, ERDC/CERL TR-15-36 (Champaign: US Army Engineer Research and Development Center, Construction Engineering Research Laboratory, University of Illinois at Urbana-Champaign, 2015).

56   See Pearl Wilcox, *The Latter Day Saints on the Missouri Frontier* (Independence, MO: pub. by author, 1972), 251; see also section 9 in the map for Mirabile Township in *Atlas of Caldwell County, Missouri* (St. Joseph, MO: Press of Lon. Hardman, 1897).

57   Ryan W. Saltzgiver, "Summary of Work at Hawn's Mill and Far West Cemetery, Northwest Missouri" (report on file at the Church History Library, Salt Lake City, Utah, 2014), 37–47.